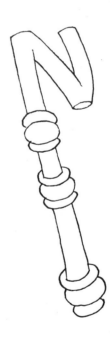

Is Noth

ing Sacred?

Gahan Wilson

St. Martin's/Marek

New York

For permission to reprint cartoons, on pages listed, I gratefully thank the following:

Fantasy & Science Fiction magazine: 13 (top), 26, 35 (top), 52, 56 (bottom), 57, 60, 61 (top), 62, 64, 68, 72, 82, 87, 88 (bottom), 89, 91, 93 (both), 95, 97, 98 (both), 99, 100, 104, 115, 121 (top), 126 (bottom); *The New Yorker:* 10 (top), 15 (bottom), 17 (both), 20 (top), 23 (both), 47 (bottom), 48 (bottom), 69 (both), 75, 80 (bottom), 96 (both), 106 (top), 107 (both), 108 (top), 112 (top), 127 (bottom); *Playboy:* 7, 8, 11, 12, 18 (bottom), 21, 22, 31, 32, 37, 38, 45, 46, 53 (top), 58, 74 (top), 77, 78, 83, 84, 85, 86 (bottom), 101, 102, 109, 110, 117 (top), 123, 124.

10 9 8 7 6 5 4 3 2 1
First Edition

Library of Congress Cataloging in Publication Data

Wilson, Gahan.
  Is nothing sacred?

  1. American wit and humor, Pictorial.   I. Title.
NC1429.W5785A4   1982   741.5'973   81-14573
ISBN 0-312-43707-2   AACR2
ISBN 0-312-43708-0 (pbk.)

For Doug Kenney

"Your Honor, the defense contends its client could never
get a fair trial in this court."

"Fetch!"

"Look, what can I tell you? That's the head
of network programming."

"I'm Special Agent Kerrington, of the
F.B.I., Mr. Ently, and I just wanted
you to know that we've checked you
out and you're a good citizen."

"We're finding it hard communicating with Audrey."

10

"Is nothing sacred?"

"Still, you've got to admit our being swallowed by
a fish has its humorous aspects!"

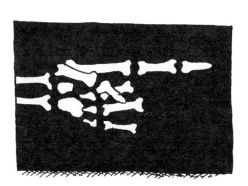

"I always knew the kid
had a lot of guts!"

"So what the hell do we do *now*?"

"I'll keep the crown, thanks."

"Didn't everybody used to have faces?"

"Now, frankly, Ed—what's all this talk about your being a fascist?"

"Not good!"

"We've worked out a little code
over the years."

"Look, Charley—the world changes."

"Scarsdale. It's Scarsdale again."

"It's a little eccentricity of mine—after I've beaten a man in
business, I like to have him stuffed."

"Whereas that fellow sitting on your right just
came in a couple of weeks ago."

"I'm afraid I'm past smiling and all that sort of thing."

"It's no good—I'm out here, too!"

"Seems all we ever do is complain!"

"What's all this nonsense about
capturing kings?"

"I'm sorry, but at this agency
we only handle jerks."

"There you are, you naughties!"

"My God—it's a Mouton Rothschild '67!"

"I'm home!"

"No, I wouldn't suggest appealing to his sense of human decency. I definitely would not try that."

"Something a little larger, please."

"If I could just once forget *something*!"

"This isn't going to help, Edward."

"I think I've found the trouble, Mr. Nadler!"

"I'll take that one over there
with the little smile."

"We're there."

"You are often clumsy."

"It's a bad table!"

"Somehow I thought the whole thing would be a lot classier!"

"You've been to one of those punk-rock places again, haven't you?"

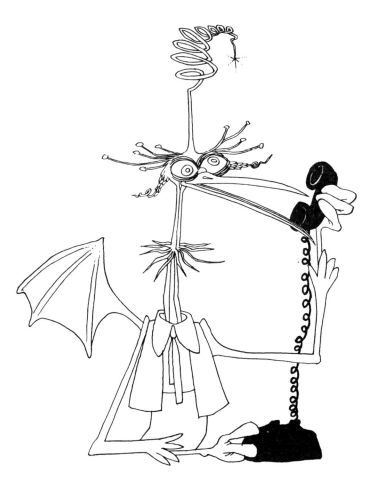

"Just who do you think
you're talking to?"

"Lord and Lady Smyth-Hadley send their regrets. General and Mrs. Markon send their regrets. Sir Oliver Pulling sends his regrets. The Duchess of Pendal sends her regrets. The Count and Countess Estervheny send their regrets. Their Royal Highnesses, Karl and Gwendolina send their regrets . . ."

"Trouble with someone like old Claude, there,
it don't matter a damn if you *do* draw first!"

"I don't know—somehow I always thought of them as
being built in factories . . ."

"I wish you'd stop asking me what
I really think, Mr. Wellsley!"

"Chestnuts! Quick! Chestnuts!"

". . . and please do hurry!"

"Of course, the place wouldn't seem so small if we weren't elephants."

"Somehow, somewhere along the line, this town lost its pride."

"Look, Mr. Tompkins, there is simply nothing
I can do for you after you're dead!"

"I think we may be just the store for you, sir!"

"You fool! There's no more of me! That's
it! I'm the last of my species!"

"Of course, none of us around here is
actually *looking forward*
to Armageddon."

"We all seem to be converging!"

"Arnold has promised to put me into the
compost pile when I die."

"I don't know . . . all I see lately
is this big, glass ball . . ."

"But of course *Dublish Torte* make you sick, sir.
Dublish Torte supposed to make you sick!"

". . . and here's to *you,* little fellow!"

"Nothing personal, Dad, but if I were you, I wouldn't ask too many questions about my boy's club."

"There's nothing anywhere says I have to go around wearing black!"

"... and now, before I sign off what the folks
here at the station say must be the last show in
the series, I'd like to thank all you loyal
viewers out there who were such a great
help to this show!"

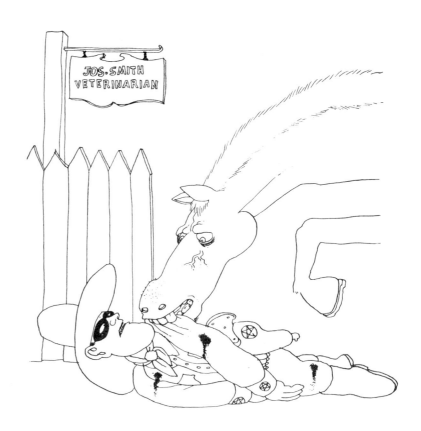

"No, big fellow, you must take me
to a *people* doctor!"

"You call *those* hopes and dreams?"

"How long has it been, Doctor, since we
had our little disagreement?"

"This is the place, driver."

"Of course, once the plague's done, we're both out of a job."

"Of course, their programming's not aimed at us!"

". . . But, then, I'm afraid youth
would be wasted on us, too."

"Now just a goddamn minute!"

". . . and this is *my* little woman."

"You just can't get into the L. A. thing,
can you, kid?"

"The hell with *this* stuff!"

"Fool!"

"I don't like the looks of your face, Mac!"

"Hold it, Charlie."

"So far, all the tests indicate, as we feared, that
you *are* a cocker spaniel."

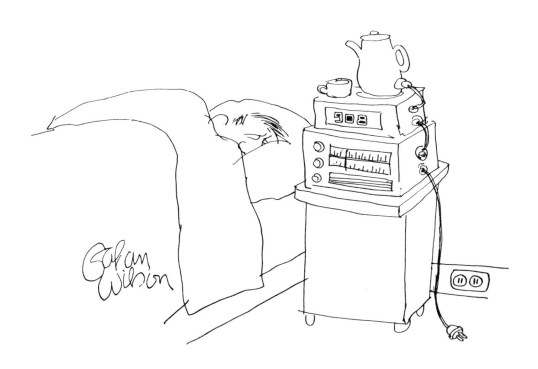

"You won't *believe* what those bastards
have dreamed up!"

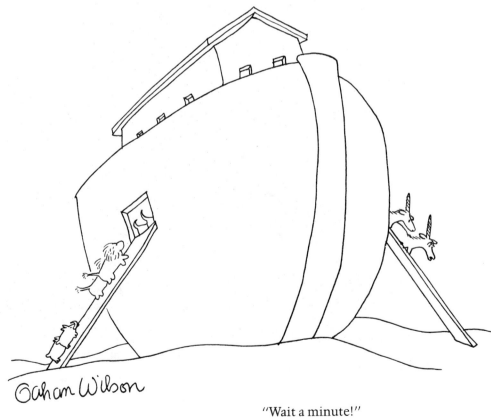

"Wait a minute!"

"Here comes another!"

"Over here, for God's sake!"

"Hello, this is, ah, Mr. Rogers speaking."

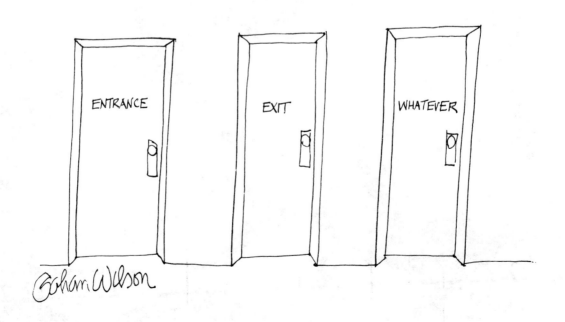

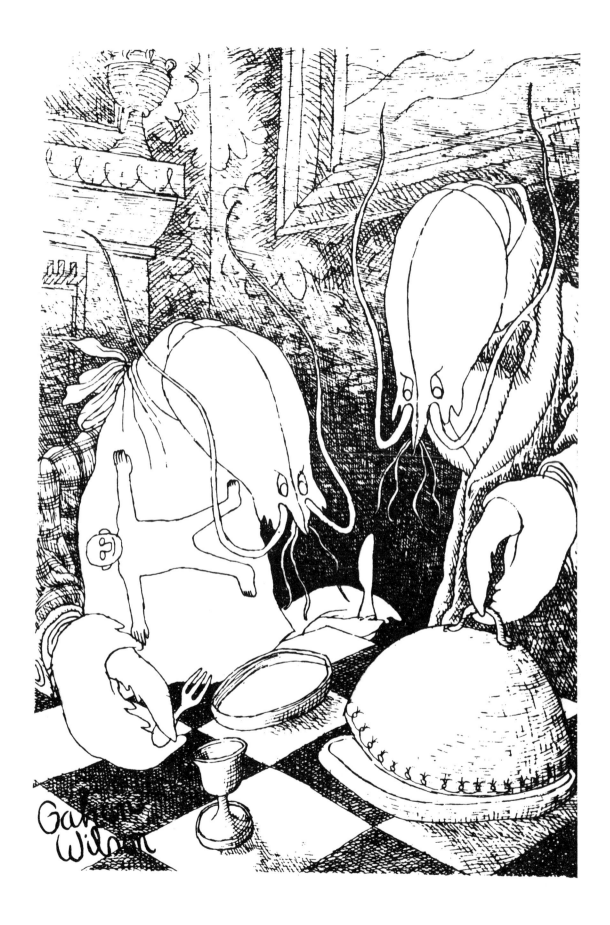

72

"Something really strange is
going on upstate!"

"I tell you, Mr. Arthur, this survey has no
way of registering a non-verbal response!"

"I'd say it's pretty obvious you've
got the wrong address, mister!"

"I'd say in that outfit you can handle just about anything Mother Nature
dishes out, Mr. Harper!"

"Forgive me, but my people often
find yours cold and distant!"

"My God—you don't mean
it's *still* 1935?"

"Oh-Oh!"

"To tell the truth, I wish this place hadn't
caught on with the werewolves!"

"I don't know why I keep thinking
it's Wednesday!"

"Congratulations, Barker, you've created life in a test tube. Of course, now you'll have to worry about dental bills, then there'll be the college expenses, and further down the line, caterers for the wedding . . ."

"Do you want the suit you came in, sir, or shall I have it destroyed?"

"I don't know, Professor, this civilization is so primitive,
it hardly seems worth our time!"

"You know, he's not really such a bad fellow once you get a couple of drinks in him!"

"You're not thinking intergalactic, Olson!"

"Er, driver, just let me off right here, please!"

"I understand it's an exact copy of a
very bad restaurant in Paris."

"We're city little people, lady, if it's
any of your damn business."

"I've told you once, I've told you a hundred times,
Bukchneck, *keep your mouth closed*!"

"Sorry I'm not making myself clearer,
but it's hard to express yourself in a
language as crude and primitive as ours."

"Alright, then—*now* what are you going to do?"

"What do you say, just this once,
to hell with Capistrano?"

"Hello, Room Service?"

"Where were you for all those years?"

"This is it, men—*the big one!*"

"He hasn't touched a thing for weeks!"

"I just don't understand it, Captain. Equal shares
of food and water to all, yet those two thrive while
we wither away."

"By God, will you look at that—
even littler people!"

"I suppose part of the
problem is we're all
Capricorns."

"That's tone control. The volume's up there."

"We knew your place would be hard to believe."

"We're a pretty folksy bunch around here, Hunter, and that's
how we'd like you to be. Folksy."

"I figure everybody else is doing it."

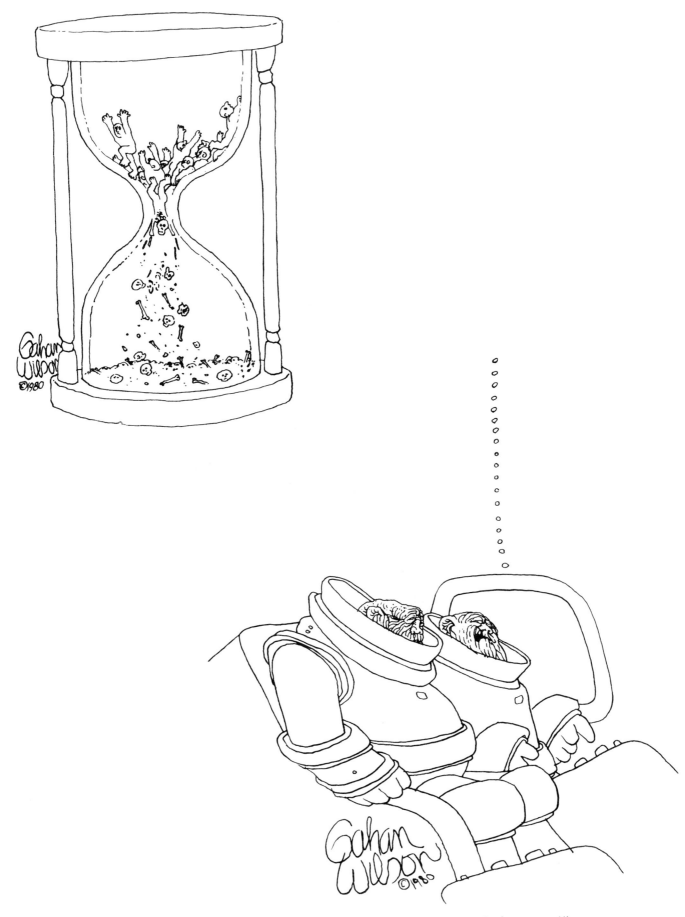

"Well, it won't be long, now!"

"It's this nutsy right hemisphere of mine!"

"Harriet? You'll never guess who's here!"

"Yes, I must admit I've done rather well here."

Gahan
Wilson

"Our people have many sayings on
the vanity of haste, effendi . . ."

"It's me!"

"Over there."

"They didn't *used* to behave like that!"

"And you, sir—have you a request
for our strolling whistler?"

"See? It's not as if you were the only one."

"Try again."

"Check it out!"

"Any time Christmas falls on the full moon—we've got problems!"

"HELP!!!"

"Wow—what do you make of *that*?!"

"What do you think, hah? Think we're *it*?!"

"I know this will be a disappointment to you, Mr. Barton,
but you're in excellent health and will probably live
for many, many years to come."

"Are you coasting again, Parker?"

"You understand you're the sort of person
I ordinarily wouldn't even speak to."

"Hello! You have reached the number of Harold Mayberry. I am sorry, but Mr. Mayberry is not in. I am a simulation of Mr. Mayberry. Please leave your name and number and Mr. Mayberry will call you back when he gets in. Thank you very much!"

"Our little joke!"

"And every day it's costing more and more!"

"O.K., remember, now—you're this giant."

"Excuse me, sir, I can't quite
make out what you're saying."

". . . and, for what it's worth, my blessing."

"Life is like . . . ah . . . life is . . . uhm . . . like . . . er . . .
life is like a dream!"

"Is this yours?"

"We really are having awful luck on this trip!"

"What's the rush?"

"Oh, believe me, *everyone's* very pleased you're here, sir!"

"But seriously, folks . . ."

"I just hope he doesn't grow up and join
some strange religious cult!"

"Harry, I wish you'd stop *doing* that!"   125

"I guess this is a pretty busy
time of year for you guys!"

"You never know when he'll
fall off the wagon."

"Look, Mr. Gurney, let's not kid ourselves.
Crazy is crazy."

"Ha ha Bill."
"Ha ha George."
"Ha ha. And here's Harry ha ha with the sports.
Ha ha Harry."
"Ha ha George."

About the Author

GAHAN WILSON says, "I was born dead and this helped my career almost as much as being the nephew of a lion tamer and a descendant of P. T. Barnum." The first confessed cartoonist to graduate from the Art Institute of Chicago, Wilson has shown at galleries in New York and San Francisco, and his genius for humor has been likened by critics to that of Swift, Gogol and Twain. He and his wife, novelist-journalist Nancy Winters, live in New York City and Connecticut.

GAHAN WILSON'S work also appears in *The New Yorker, Paris Match, Playboy, Punch, The National Lampoon,* and *The New York Times.*